MW00874838

THE COMPLETE 2024 LOW OXALATE DIET COOKBOOK

100+ Delicious Nutritional Recipes to Reduce Inflammation, Prevent Kidney Stones and Improve Overall Health Standard

LUCKY WILSON

Copyright © 2024 by Lucky Wilson

All rights reserved. No part of this publication may be reproduced, distributed, or transmitted in any form or by any means, including photocopying, recording, or other electronic or mechanical methods, without the prior written permission of the publisher, except in the case of brief quotation embodied in critical reviews and certain other noncommercial uses permitted by copyright law.

Table of Contents

3

WELCOME TO LOW OXALATE DIET.........

INTRODUCTION

Introduction to the Low Oxalate Diet

This dietary approach focuses on managing the intake of oxalates, natural compounds found in many plant-based foods that can impact kidney health and certain medical conditions. The essence of the Low Oxalate diet lies in reducing the consumption of foods rich in oxalates, which are known to contribute to the formation of kidney stones in susceptible individuals. By adopting this diet, individuals aim to lower the risk of kidney stone recurrence and manage conditions like hyperoxaluria more effectively.

Beyond kidney stone prevention, this diet holds potential benefits for those managing other health challenges influenced by oxalates, such as gastrointestinal disorders and specific types of kidney disease. By carefully selecting foods lower in oxalates and integrating them into a balanced diet, individuals can support overall health and potentially alleviate related symptoms.

Getting started with the Low Oxalate diet involves familiarizing oneself with foods categorized by their oxalate content. High oxalate foods include spinach, nuts, chocolate, and certain whole grains, while low oxalate alternatives include most fruits, dairy products, lean meats, and specific vegetables like cabbage and bell peppers.

Throughout this cookbook, you'll discover practical guidance on meal planning, delicious recipes crafted with low oxalate ingredients, and insights into maintaining a balanced lifestyle while managing oxalate intake. Whether you're exploring this diet for preventive health measures or managing specific health conditions, this introduction sets the stage for a journey towards improved well-being through informed dietary choices.

What is Low Oxalate Diet

A low oxalate diet is a dietary approach that involves reducing the intake of foods high in oxalates, which are natural compounds found in many plant-based foods. Oxalates can bind with calcium in the body to form crystals, and in some individuals, these crystals can lead to the formation of kidney stones. Therefore, a low oxalate diet aims to minimize the risk of kidney stone formation and manage conditions such as hyperoxaluria. Foods that are typically high in oxalates include spinach, rhubarb, almonds, chocolate, and certain beans. On the other hand, low oxalate foods include most fruits, dairy products, lean meats, and specific vegetables like cabbage, cauliflower, and bell peppers. The diet involves careful selection of foods to limit oxalate intake while maintaining a balanced nutritional profile. It may be recommended for individuals who have a history of kidney stones or certain kidney conditions, or those who experience symptoms exacerbated by high oxalate intake, such as certain gastrointestinal disorders.

Purpose of Low Oxalate Diet

A low oxalate diet serves multiple crucial purposes in promoting kidney health and managing conditions exacerbated by oxalates. Oxalates are naturally occurring compounds found in many plant-based foods that, when consumed in excess, can crystallize and accumulate in the kidneys, potentially leading to kidney stone formation and aggravating various health conditions. By adopting a low oxalate diet, individuals can mitigate these risks and optimize their overall health.

1. Promoting Kidney Health: The primary goal of a low oxalate diet is to promote kidney health by reducing the intake of oxalate-rich foods. For individuals prone to kidney stones or managing conditions like hyperoxaluria, limiting dietary oxalates can significantly decrease the formation of oxalate crystals in the kidneys. This proactive dietary approach not only aims to prevent kidney stone recurrence but also supports optimal kidney function over the long term, reducing the burden on this vital organ and promoting overall urinary tract health.

2. Managing Oxalate-Related Conditions: Beyond kidney stones, certain health conditions are exacerbated by oxalates. Conditions such as vulvodynia, interstitial cystitis, and autism spectrum disorders have been linked to increased sensitivity to oxalates. A low oxalate diet can help manage symptoms associated with these conditions by reducing oxalate intake and alleviating inflammation or irritation caused by oxalate deposits. By providing relief from these symptoms, individuals can improve their quality of life and better manage their health challenges.

3. Preventing Oxalate-Related Complications: In addition to kidney stones and specific health conditions, a low oxalate diet plays a preventive role in reducing the risk of oxalate-related complications. High oxalate levels in the body can contribute to the formation of crystals not only in the kidneys but also in other organs and tissues. By controlling dietary oxalate intake, individuals can lower their risk of developing complications such as oxalate nephropathy, a condition where oxalate crystals accumulate in the kidneys and cause damage over time.

4. Enhancing Nutritional Awareness and Balance: Educating individuals about oxalate content in foods and

promoting balanced nutrition is another important aspect of a low oxalate diet. While reducing oxalate intake, it is essential to maintain adequate intake of other essential nutrients like calcium, magnesium, and vitamin C. This dietary approach encourages mindfulness about food choices and empowers individuals to make informed decisions that support overall health and well-being.

Benefits of a Low Oxalate Diet

A low oxalate diet offers numerous potential benefits, ranging from reducing the formation of kidney stones to alleviating symptoms of certain health conditions and promoting overall well-being. Oxalates are naturally occurring compounds found in many plant-based foods that can crystallize and accumulate in the kidneys, leading to kidney stone formation and exacerbating various health conditions. By moderating oxalate intake through dietary adjustments, individuals can experience significant improvements in their health outcomes.

1. Reducing Kidney Stone Formation: One of the primary benefits of a low oxalate diet is its effectiveness in reducing the formation of kidney stones. Kidney stones, which are solid masses of crystals that form in the kidneys, can cause severe pain and discomfort. By limiting dietary oxalates, individuals can decrease the amount of oxalate available for crystal formation in the kidneys, thereby lowering the risk of developing kidney stones. This proactive approach not only helps prevent stone recurrence but also supports overall kidney health by reducing strain on the kidneys.

2. Alleviating Symptoms of Oxalate-Related Conditions: Beyond kidney stones, certain health conditions are exacerbated by high oxalate levels. Conditions such as vulvodynia, interstitial cystitis, and autism spectrum disorders have been linked to increased sensitivity to oxalates, leading to symptoms such as pain, inflammation, and urinary discomfort. Adopting a low oxalate diet can help alleviate these symptoms by reducing oxalate intake and minimizing the impact of oxalate crystals on affected tissues. This dietary modification may provide relief and improve quality of life for individuals managing these conditions.

3. Supporting Gut Health and Absorption of Nutrients: High oxalate intake has been associated with gastrointestinal issues, including digestive discomfort and impaired nutrient absorption. By reducing dietary oxalates, individuals may experience improvements in gut health, including reduced bloating, gas, and other digestive symptoms. Furthermore, a low oxalate diet supports the absorption of essential nutrients like calcium and magnesium, which are crucial for bone health and overall well-being. This nutritional balance contributes to better overall health outcomes and enhances the body's ability to utilize important vitamins and minerals.

4. Promoting Overall Well-being: In addition to specific health benefits, adopting a low oxalate diet can contribute to overall well-being by promoting mindful eating habits and dietary awareness. By focusing on nutrient-dense foods low in oxalates, individuals are encouraged to make health-conscious choices that support long-term health goals. This dietary approach fosters a sense of empowerment and control over one's health, leading to improved energy levels, mood stability, and overall quality of life.

Understanding Low Oxalate Diet: Foods to Eat

A low oxalate diet is a dietary approach aimed at reducing the intake of oxalate-rich foods to manage conditions exacerbated by oxalates and to promote kidney health. Oxalates are naturally occurring compounds found in many plant-based foods that can crystallize and accumulate in the kidneys, potentially leading to kidney stone formation and aggravating certain health conditions. By incorporating foods low in oxalates into your diet, you can effectively support kidney health and overall well-being.

Fruits

Apples: Apples are a versatile fruit low in oxalates, making them an excellent choice for snacks, desserts, or as an addition to salads. Their natural sweetness and crisp texture make them enjoyable both raw and cooked.

1. Berries: Strawberries, blueberries, and raspberries are low oxalate fruits rich in antioxidants and fiber. They can be added to yogurt, oatmeal, smoothies, or enjoyed on their own as a refreshing snack.

2. Pears: Pears are another low oxalate option that can be eaten fresh, sliced into salads, or baked for a delicious dessert. They provide a sweet and juicy flavor while contributing to your daily fruit intake.

Vegetables

Leafy Greens: While spinach and Swiss chard are high in oxalates and best consumed in moderation, alternatives like kale, collard greens, and lettuce varieties are lower in oxalates and provide essential nutrients like vitamins A, C, and K. These greens can be used in salads, smoothies, soups, or sautéed as a side dish.

1. Cruciferous Vegetables: Broccoli, cauliflower, and Brussels sprouts are nutrient-dense vegetables low in oxalates. They are rich in fiber, vitamins,
2. and minerals, making them excellent choices for roasting, steaming, or adding to stir-fries and casseroles.Bell Peppers: Colorful and versatile, bell peppers are low oxalate vegetables that can be enjoyed raw in salads, stuffed with lean protein and grains, or roasted as a

flavorful side dish. They provide vitamin C and antioxidants to support immune function and overall health.

Grains and Starches

1. Quinoa: Quinoa is a nutritious whole grain alternative that is naturally low in oxalates. It is gluten-free and provides complete protein, making it a valuable addition to salads, soups, or served as a side dish with vegetables and lean proteins.

2. Oats: Whole oats or oatmeal are low oxalate grains that offer fiber and help support digestive health. They can be enjoyed as a warm breakfast cereal with fruits and nuts, incorporated into baked goods, or used as a binding agent in meatballs and veggie burgers.

3. Rice: White rice and brown rice are staple grains that are low in oxalates and provide energy-sustaining carbohydrates. They serve as a versatile base for main dishes, stir-fries, pilafs, or can be used in rice-based desserts and puddings.

Proteins

Lean Meats: Chicken, turkey, and lean cuts of beef or pork are low oxalate sources of high-quality protein. They can be grilled, baked, or sautéed with herbs and spices to create flavorful and satisfying meals that support muscle growth and repair.

1. Fish: Salmon, trout, and white fish varieties are low oxalate choices rich in omega-3 fatty acids, which support heart health and cognitive function. These fish can be grilled, baked, or pan-seared and served with vegetables and whole grains for a balanced meal.

2. Eggs: Eggs are a versatile and nutrient-dense food that is naturally low in oxalates. They can be prepared in various ways, including scrambled, poached, boiled, or used as an ingredient in omelets, frittatas, and baked goods.

Dairy
Cheese: Hard cheeses such as cheddar, mozzarella, and Swiss are generally lower in oxalates compared to soft cheeses. They add flavor and richness to dishes and can be grated, sliced, or melted over vegetables and pasta dishes.

1. Milk and Yogurt: Dairy products contain calcium, which can bind to oxalates in the digestive tract and reduce their absorption. Opt for lower oxalate choices like Greek yogurt or lactose-free milk to enjoy the benefits of dairy while managing oxalate intake.

Nuts and Seeds

Almonds: Almonds are a low oxalate nut that provides healthy fats, protein, and fiber. They can be enjoyed raw, roasted, or ground into almond flour for baking recipes and gluten-free alternatives.

1. Sunflower Seeds: Sunflower seeds are low in oxalates and rich in vitamin E, magnesium, and selenium. They can be sprinkled on salads, yogurt, or enjoyed as a snack on their own.

Beverages

1. Water: Staying hydrated with water is essential for kidney health and overall well-being. Drinking an adequate

amount of water throughout the day helps flush out toxins and prevent kidney stone formation.

2. Herbal Teas: Herbal teas such as chamomile, peppermint, and ginger are caffeine-free options that can be enjoyed hot or cold. They provide hydration and offer soothing properties that promote relaxation and digestive health.

Basics of Low Oxalate Diet: Balancing Nutrition and Minimizing Oxalate Consumption

A low oxalate diet is a dietary approach aimed at reducing the intake of oxalate-rich foods to manage conditions exacerbated by oxalates and promote kidney health. Oxalates are naturally occurring compounds found in many plant-based foods that can crystallize and accumulate in the kidneys, potentially leading to kidney stone formation and aggravating certain health conditions. By understanding the principles and guidelines of a low oxalate diet, individuals can effectively optimize their nutrition while minimizing oxalate consumption.

Introduction to Oxalates and Health

Oxalates are substances found in a wide range of foods, particularly in plant-based sources such as fruits, vegetables, nuts, seeds, grains, and legumes. While some oxalates are necessary for normal bodily functions, excessive intake can lead to health issues, especially for individuals prone to kidney stones or managing conditions exacerbated by oxalates. Adopting a low oxalate diet involves identifying high-oxalate foods and making informed dietary choices to reduce oxalate intake without compromising overall nutritional balance.

Principles of a Low Oxalate Diet

1. Awareness of High-Oxalate Foods: The foundation of a low oxalate diet begins with identifying and avoiding foods that are high in oxalates. This includes spinach, Swiss chard, beets, rhubarb, and certain nuts and seeds. By limiting these foods, individuals can lower their overall

oxalate intake and reduce the risk of oxalate-related complications.

2. Emphasis on Variety and Balance: While reducing oxalate intake, it's crucial to maintain a diverse and balanced diet. Incorporate a wide range of low oxalate fruits, vegetables, grains, proteins, and dairy products to ensure adequate nutrition. Opt for alternatives like kale, broccoli, quinoa, lean meats, and low oxalate dairy to support overall health and well-being.

3. Cooking Methods to Reduce Oxalate Content: Certain cooking methods can help reduce oxalate levels in foods. Steaming, boiling, or soaking vegetables and grains before cooking can help leach out oxalates, making them more suitable for a low oxalate diet. Experiment with different culinary techniques to maximize flavor while minimizing oxalate content.

4. Consider Calcium and Oxalate Interaction: Consuming foods rich in calcium along with oxalate-containing foods can help reduce oxalate absorption in the digestive tract. Incorporate low oxalate sources of calcium such as dairy products, fortified plant-based milks, and leafy greens to support bone health and mitigate oxalate-related risks.

Guidelines for Implementing a Low Oxalate Diet

1. Start Gradually: Transitioning to a low oxalate diet can be a gradual process. Begin by identifying high-oxalate foods in your current diet and gradually replacing them with lower oxalate alternatives. This approach allows for adjustments while maintaining nutritional balance.

2. Monitor Portion Sizes: Pay attention to portion sizes of foods that are moderate in oxalates. While some foods may be low in oxalates individually, consuming large quantities can still contribute to overall oxalate intake. Practice portion control to manage oxalate consumption effectively.

3. Read Labels and Recipes: When following a low oxalate diet, it's essential to read food labels and recipes carefully. Be aware of hidden sources of oxalates in processed foods, sauces, and condiments. Choose homemade meals using fresh ingredients to have better control over oxalate content.

4. Stay Hydrated: Adequate hydration is crucial for kidney health and can help prevent kidney stone formation. Drink plenty of water throughout the day to dilute urine and reduce the concentration of oxalates in the kidneys. Herbal

teas and diluted fruit juices can also contribute to hydration without excessive oxalate intake.

Practical Tips for Success

1. Consult with a Healthcare Provider: Before starting a low oxalate diet, consult with a healthcare provider or registered dietitian. They can provide personalized recommendations based on your health status, dietary preferences, and specific needs.

2. Keep a Food Diary: Track your dietary intake and symptoms to monitor the effects of a low oxalate diet on your health. A food diary can help identify triggers, assess nutrient intake, and make adjustments as needed to optimize outcomes.

3. Educate Yourself: Stay informed about oxalate content in foods and ongoing research related to oxalate-related conditions. Attend educational seminars, read reputable sources, and join support groups to exchange experiences and gain insights into managing a low oxalate diet effectively.

Causes of Oxalate Buildup

Oxalate buildup in the body, leading to conditions such as kidney stones, can be influenced by various factors, including dietary sources, medical conditions, and metabolic processes. Understanding these causes is crucial for managing and preventing oxalate-related health issues.

Dietary Sources

High-Oxalate Foods:

1. Spinach and Swiss Chard: These leafy greens are among the highest in oxalates. Consuming large quantities can significantly increase oxalate levels in the body.

2. Beets and Beet Greens: Both the roots and the leaves of beets are rich in oxalates, making them a notable contributor to oxalate buildup.

3. Nuts and Seeds: Almonds, cashews, and sesame seeds are high in oxalates. Regular consumption can contribute to higher oxalate levels.

4. Rhubarb: This plant is exceptionally high in oxalates, particularly in its stalks, and can significantly impact oxalate accumulation.

5. Chocolate and Cocoa: Both are rich in oxalates. Frequent consumption of chocolate-based products can contribute to oxalate buildup.

Oxalate-Rich Beverages:

1. Tea: Black tea, in particular, contains high levels of oxalates. Drinking large amounts can increase oxalate levels in the body.

2. Certain Juices: Juices made from high-oxalate fruits and vegetables, such as cranberry juice and beet juice, can also contribute to oxalate buildup.

Processed Foods:

1. Many processed foods contain hidden sources of oxalates, including certain snacks, cereals, and pre-packaged meals. Ingredients like soy and certain preservatives can elevate oxalate content.

Medical Conditions

Hyperoxaluria:

1. Primary Hyperoxaluria: A rare genetic disorder causing the liver to produce an excess amount of oxalate. This condition leads to a significant increase in oxalate levels in the body.

2. Secondary Hyperoxaluria: Often resulting from dietary factors, certain gastrointestinal disorders, or an overuse of vitamin C supplements, which the body converts to oxalates.

Malabsorption Syndromes:

1. Inflammatory Bowel Disease (IBD): Conditions like Crohn's disease and ulcerative colitis can impair the intestines' ability to absorb nutrients, including calcium, which binds to oxalate. Reduced calcium absorption increases free oxalate in the intestines, leading to higher oxalate absorption into the bloodstream.

2. Short Bowel Syndrome: This condition, resulting from surgical removal of portions of the intestines, can lead to malabsorption and increased oxalate absorption.

Chronic Antibiotic Use:

1. Prolonged use of antibiotics can disrupt the gut microbiota, reducing populations of beneficial bacteria like Oxalobacter formigenes, which degrade oxalates in the intestines. This disruption can lead to increased oxalate absorption.

Metabolic Factors

Vitamin C Metabolism:

1. Excessive intake of vitamin C (ascorbic acid) can lead to increased oxalate production, as the body metabolizes vitamin C into oxalates. While moderate vitamin C intake is essential for health, megadoses can contribute to oxalate buildup.

Calcium Imbalance:

1. Calcium binds with oxalates in the intestines, forming an insoluble compound that is excreted in the stool. When dietary calcium is insufficient, more free oxalate is available for absorption, leading to higher oxalate levels in the bloodstream and urine.

Fat Malabsorption:

1. Conditions that cause fat malabsorption, such as chronic pancreatitis or celiac disease, can lead to increased oxalate absorption. Unabsorbed fatty acids bind with calcium, reducing the availability of calcium to bind with oxalates. This increases the amount of free oxalate available for absorption.

Genetic Predisposition

Genetic Mutations:

1. Certain genetic mutations can affect oxalate metabolism, leading to increased oxalate production or reduced oxalate degradation. For example, mutations in the AGXT gene cause primary hyperoxaluria type 1, resulting in overproduction of oxalates.

Dietary Imbalances

Low Calcium Intake:

1. Adequate dietary calcium is crucial for binding oxalates in the intestines, preventing their absorption into the

bloodstream. Diets low in calcium can lead to increased oxalate absorption and higher oxalate levels in the body.

High Protein Diets:

1. High protein intake, particularly from animal sources, can increase the risk of kidney stones, including oxalate stones. Proteins can increase calcium excretion in the urine and reduce urinary citrate, a compound that inhibits stone formation.

Lifestyle Factors

Dehydration:

1. Inadequate fluid intake can lead to concentrated urine, which increases the risk of oxalate crystallization and kidney stone formation. Staying well-hydrated helps dilute oxalates in the urine, reducing the risk of stone formation.

High Salt Intake:

1. Excessive sodium intake can increase calcium excretion in the urine, leading to a higher risk of calcium oxalate

stone formation. Reducing salt intake can help manage oxalate levels and reduce the risk of kidney stones.

Gut Microbiota

1. Reduced Oxalate-Degrading Bacteria: The presence of certain gut bacteria, such as Oxalobacter formigenes, is essential for degrading oxalates in the intestines. Factors that reduce these beneficial bacteria, such as antibiotic use or dietary imbalances, can lead to increased oxalate absorption.

2. Probiotic Supplementation: Some studies suggest that probiotic supplements containing oxalate-degrading bacteria can help reduce oxalate absorption and lower oxalate levels in the body.

Methods to Reduce Oxalate Levels

Reducing oxalate levels in the diet is crucial for individuals prone to kidney stones or other health issues exacerbated by oxalate accumulation. Effective strategies and practical tips can help lower oxalate intake while maintaining a balanced and nutritious diet. This guide explores various methods, including cooking techniques and food preparation strategies, to minimize oxalate levels.

Cooking Methods

1. Boiling: Boiling vegetables can significantly reduce their oxalate content. During boiling, oxalates leach into the cooking water, which is then discarded. This method is particularly effective for high-oxalate vegetables like spinach, beets, and Swiss chard. For best results, boil vegetables in plenty of water and avoid using the cooking water in other dishes.

2. Steaming: Steaming is another effective way to reduce oxalates, although it is slightly less effective than boiling.

Steaming helps preserve nutrients while reducing oxalate levels, making it a good option for vegetables like broccoli, carrots, and kale. Ensure that the vegetables are well-cooked to maximize oxalate reduction.

3. Soaking: Soaking foods like grains, beans, and nuts before cooking can help reduce their oxalate content. Soaking allows oxalates to dissolve in water, which is then drained away. For example, soaking beans overnight and rinsing them thoroughly before cooking can lower their oxalate levels. Similarly, soaking nuts before consumption or blending can make them less oxalate-dense.

4. Blanching: Blanching involves briefly boiling vegetables and then plunging them into ice water to stop the cooking process. This method can help reduce oxalate content while preserving the texture and color of vegetables. Blanching is particularly useful for leafy greens and other high-oxalate vegetables that you may want to use in salads or other dishes.

Food Preparation Techniques

1. Pairing with Calcium-Rich Foods: Consuming oxalate-containing foods with calcium-rich foods can help reduce oxalate absorption in the digestive tract. Calcium binds with oxalates to form insoluble compounds that are excreted in the stool. For instance, pairing spinach with a calcium-rich dairy product like cheese or yogurt can mitigate oxalate absorption. This strategy is beneficial for managing overall oxalate levels in the body.

2. Using Low-Oxalate Ingredients: Substituting high-oxalate foods with low-oxalate alternatives is an effective way to reduce oxalate intake. For example, replace high-oxalate leafy greens like spinach and Swiss chard with lower-oxalate options like kale, bok choy, or lettuce. Opt for white rice or quinoa instead of high-oxalate grains like whole wheat or brown rice.

3. Blending and Juicing Carefully: Blending and juicing can concentrate oxalates if high-oxalate foods are used. When making smoothies or juices, choose low-oxalate fruits and vegetables, such as cucumbers, apples, and berries. If using high-oxalate ingredients, balance them with low-oxalate counterparts and add a source of calcium,

such as almond milk or a dollop of yogurt, to reduce oxalate absorption.

Additional Practical Tips

1. Hydration: Staying well-hydrated is crucial for reducing oxalate buildup in the kidneys. Drinking plenty of water helps dilute oxalates in the urine, reducing the risk of kidney stone formation. Aim to drink at least 8-10 glasses of water daily, and more if you engage in physical activity or live in a hot climate.

2. Reading Labels: Processed and packaged foods can contain hidden sources of oxalates. Read food labels carefully to identify and avoid products with high-oxalate ingredients. Be cautious of snacks, cereals, and condiments that may contribute to increased oxalate intake.

3. Moderation: While it's important to reduce high-oxalate foods, complete elimination may not be necessary. Focus on moderation and balance, incorporating a variety of low-oxalate foods into your diet. Monitoring portion sizes of moderate oxalate foods can also help manage overall oxalate intake.

Measuring Oxalate Content: Tools and Techniques for Informed Dietary Choices

Understanding and managing oxalate intake is essential for individuals prone to kidney stones or other oxalate-related health issues. Accurate measurement of oxalate content in foods helps individuals make informed dietary choices. This guide provides insights into how oxalate content is measured in foods and the tools available to assist in this process.

Methods for Measuring Oxalate Content

Chemical Analysis:

1. Ion Chromatography: This advanced technique separates oxalates from other compounds in food samples. The process involves extracting oxalates from food, passing the extract through an ion exchange column, and measuring the oxalate concentration using a detector. Ion chromatography provides highly accurate and precise results, making it a

standard method in scientific research and food testing laboratories.

2. High-Performance Liquid Chromatography (HPLC): HPLC is another sophisticated method used to quantify oxalate content. It involves dissolving food samples in a solvent, filtering the solution, and injecting it into an HPLC system. The oxalates are separated and measured based on their interaction with the column and detector. HPLC is widely used for its accuracy and reliability in determining oxalate levels.

Enzymatic Assays:

Enzymatic assays utilize specific enzymes to break down oxalates into measurable products. These assays are often used in research and clinical settings due to their simplicity and specificity. The enzyme oxalate oxidase, for example, catalyzes the conversion of oxalates into carbon dioxide and hydrogen peroxide, which can then be quantified. While not as precise as chromatographic methods, enzymatic assays offer a practical and cost-effective alternative for routine testing.

Tools for Informed Dietary Choices

1. Food Composition Databases: Several comprehensive food composition databases provide detailed information on the oxalate content of various foods. These databases are compiled from scientific literature and laboratory analyses. Notable examples include the USDA National Nutrient Database and specialized databases like the Harvard Oxalate Database. Accessing these resources allows individuals to identify low-oxalate food options and plan balanced diets accordingly.

2. Mobile Apps and Online Tools: Technology has made it easier than ever to access information on oxalate content. Mobile apps and online tools, such as the "Oxalate Calculator" or "Oxalate Food Guide," offer user-friendly interfaces for searching and comparing the oxalate levels in different foods. These tools often include features like meal planning, tracking, and personalized recommendations, making them valuable resources for managing oxalate intake on the go.

3. Professional Guidance: Consulting with healthcare professionals, such as registered dietitians or nutritionists, can provide personalized guidance on managing oxalate

intake. These experts have access to the latest research and resources, enabling them to offer tailored advice based on individual health needs and dietary preferences. Regular consultations can help individuals make informed choices and adjust their diets to optimize health outcomes.

Practical Tips for Measuring and Managing Oxalate Intake

1. Prioritize Low-Oxalate Foods: When planning meals, prioritize foods known to be low in oxalates. Examples include most fruits (except berries), certain vegetables (like cucumbers and zucchini), and grains like white rice and quinoa. Using food composition databases and apps can help identify these options easily.

2. Moderation and Balance: While it's essential to reduce high-oxalate foods, complete elimination is often unnecessary. Focus on moderation and balance, incorporating a variety of low-oxalate foods into your diet. Monitor portion sizes of moderate-oxalate foods to manage overall intake effectively.

3. Cooking Techniques: Utilize cooking methods that reduce oxalate content, such as boiling and steaming, to prepare high-oxalate vegetables. Discarding the cooking water can further decrease oxalate levels in the final dish.

4. Stay Hydrated: Adequate hydration helps dilute oxalates in the urine, reducing the risk of kidney stone formation. Aim to drink plenty of water throughout the day, especially if you consume higher oxalate foods occasionally.

Preventing Kidney Stones

Kidney stones are a common and painful health issue that can significantly impact quality of life. One of the most effective strategies for preventing kidney stones, particularly those composed of calcium oxalate, is adopting a low oxalate diet. By reducing urinary oxalate excretion and promoting proper hydration, individuals can greatly decrease their risk of developing kidney stones. This discussion explores the role of a low oxalate diet in kidney stone prevention and offers practical advice for maintaining kidney health.

The Role of Oxalates in Kidney Stone Formation

Oxalates are naturally occurring compounds found in many foods. When consumed, oxalates can bind with calcium in the urine to form calcium oxalate crystals. These crystals can aggregate into stones, leading to the formation of kidney stones. High oxalate levels in the urine significantly increase the risk of kidney stone development.

Benefits of a Low Oxalate Diet

1. Reducing Urinary Oxalate Excretion: A low oxalate diet directly reduces the amount of oxalate available to form stones. By limiting the intake of high-oxalate foods, individuals can lower their urinary oxalate levels, decreasing the likelihood of crystal formation. Foods high in oxalates, such as spinach, beets, nuts, and chocolate, should be consumed in moderation or avoided altogether.

2. Promoting Calcium-Oxalate Binding: Consuming adequate calcium is essential for individuals on a low oxalate diet. Calcium binds with oxalates in the intestines, forming insoluble compounds that are excreted in the stool

rather than absorbed into the bloodstream and subsequently excreted in the urine. Including calcium-rich foods in meals, such as dairy products, fortified plant milks, and certain green vegetables, can help reduce urinary oxalate levels.

Promoting Hydration

1. Increasing Fluid Intake: Proper hydration is critical for preventing kidney stones. Adequate fluid intake dilutes the urine, reducing the concentration of oxalates and other stone-forming substances. Drinking plenty of water throughout the day helps flush out potential crystal-forming compounds before they can aggregate into stones. Aim to drink at least 8-10 glasses of water daily, and more if you engage in strenuous activities or live in a hot climate.
2. Choosing the Right Beverages: While water is the best choice for hydration, other beverages can also contribute to overall fluid intake. Herbal teas, diluted fruit juices, and beverages with low or no oxalate content are suitable options. Be cautious with drinks high in oxalates, such as

black tea and certain fruit juices, as they can contribute to oxalate buildup.

Practical Tips for Preventing Kidney Stones

1. Balanced Diet: Adopting a balanced diet that includes a variety of low oxalate foods is essential. Focus on incorporating fruits, vegetables, whole grains, and lean proteins while avoiding or limiting high-oxalate foods. Maintaining a diverse and nutrient-rich diet supports overall health and reduces the risk of kidney stone formation.

2. Cooking Techniques: Utilizing cooking methods that reduce oxalate content in foods can further decrease the risk of kidney stones. Boiling high-oxalate vegetables and discarding the cooking water is an effective technique. Additionally, soaking beans, nuts, and seeds before cooking can help reduce their oxalate levels.

3. Regular Monitoring: Individuals at risk of kidney stones should regularly monitor their urinary oxalate levels through medical check-ups. Healthcare providers can offer

personalized advice and adjust dietary recommendations based on individual needs and health status.

4. Consulting with Healthcare Professionals: Working with healthcare professionals, including dietitians and nephrologists, can provide valuable guidance in managing oxalate intake and preventing kidney stones. These experts can help create tailored meal plans, offer dietary supplements if necessary, and monitor overall kidney health.

Possible Downsides of a Low Oxalate Diet

While a low oxalate diet can be beneficial for preventing kidney stones and managing oxalate-related health issues, it is not without its potential downsides. Adopting such a diet requires careful consideration to ensure it remains balanced and nutritionally adequate. Here are some key challenges and considerations associated with a low oxalate diet.

1. Restricted Food Choices: One of the primary challenges of a low oxalate diet is the restriction of many common and nutritious foods. High-oxalate foods, such as spinach, beets, nuts, chocolate, and certain grains, are often excluded or significantly limited. This restriction can make meal planning more difficult and may reduce the variety of foods available, potentially leading to a less enjoyable eating experience. The limited food choices may also make it challenging to dine out or participate in social eating situations, where high-oxalate foods might be prevalent.

2. Nutritional Adequacy: Ensuring nutritional adequacy on a low oxalate diet requires careful planning. Many high-oxalate foods are rich in essential nutrients, such as vitamins, minerals, and antioxidants. For instance, spinach is a good source of iron and calcium, while nuts provide healthy fats and protein. Excluding these foods could lead to nutrient deficiencies if not appropriately compensated. It is crucial to find alternative sources of these nutrients to maintain a balanced diet. For example, incorporating low-oxalate vegetables, fortified foods, and appropriate supplements can help address potential deficiencies.

3. Potential for Over-Reliance on Processed Foods: In an effort to avoid high-oxalate foods, some individuals may turn to processed or convenience foods that are low in oxalates but high in other undesirable components like added sugars, unhealthy fats, and sodium. This shift can undermine the overall health benefits of a low oxalate diet. It is essential to focus on whole, unprocessed foods to maintain a diet that supports overall health and well-being.

4. Social and Psychological Impact: The social and psychological impact of a restrictive diet should not be underestimated. Constantly monitoring food choices and avoiding certain foods can lead to stress and anxiety around eating. This can affect one's relationship with food and potentially lead to disordered eating patterns. Finding a balance that allows for occasional indulgences and flexibility is important for long-term adherence and mental health.

Welcome to Low Oxalate Diet............

Low Oxalate Diet Recipes

Kidney Stone Safe Energy Balls

INGREDIENTS

1. 1.5 cup of Old fashioned oats
2. 2 tbsp Lilly's stevia baking semi sweet chocolate chips
3. 1 tbsp honey
4. 1 cup of peanut butter

INSTRUCTIONS

1. In a large bowl mix all the ingredients together.
2. Roll into bite-size balls.
3. Put in pan and place in fridge to set.
4. They keep nicely in freezer and I like to put them there as I think about them less and therefore eat less.

Oat Bran Muffin

INGREDIENTS

* ¼ cup brown sugar
* 2 cups Bob Red Mill High Fiber Oat Bran Cereal (if you cannot find at store go to Amazon)
* 1 cup whole wheat flour
* 2 tablespoons ground flax meal
* 2 teaspoons baking powder
* 2 teaspoons baking soda
* ½ cup liquid egg whites
* 1 cup chilled applesauce (no sugar added)
* 3 tablespoons olive oil
* 1 ½ cups of frozen cranberries (or any berry you like)

INSTRUCTIONS

1. Preheat oven to 400 degree

2. Thoroughly mix brown sugar, oat bran cereal, whole wheat flour, flax meal, baking powder, and baking soda

3. Add eggs, applesauce, olive oil, and cranberries

4. Mix with a wooden spoon until well-blended

5. Spoon into sprayed muffin pans (sprayed with whatever spray oil you use)

6. Bake at 400 for 15 minutes

7. Let cool for 10 minutes on a baking rack

Low Oxalate Granola

INGREDIENTS

* 1.25 teaspoon vanilla extract

* 2 tablespoons vegetable oil

* 3 cups rolled old fashioned oats gluten-free if gluten intolerant

* 1.5 teaspoon ground cinnamon

* 1/2 cup unsalted sunflower seeds

* 1/2 cup unsalted pistachios

* 1/4 teaspoon kosher salt

* 2 Tablespoons sugar-free pancake syrup

* 1/2 Cup no sugar added dried cranberries

INSTRUCTIONS

1. Preheat oven to 325 degrees.

2. In a large bowl, combine oats, sunflower seeds, dried cranberries, pistachios, oil, pancake syrup, and vanilla extract. Stir together with a spatula until evenly mixed.

3. Add in the cinnamon and salt, mix together.

4. Line a baking sheet with parchment paper and lightly spray with cooking spray.

5. Pour granola onto the baking sheet, making sure it's evenly distributed.

6. Bake for 10 minutes, then stir, bake another 5 minutes, until golden brown.

7. Remove and let cool.

Low-Oxalate Green Superfood Soup

Ingredients

* 10 cups bone broth preferably homemade

* 2 tablespoons Wildly Organic Butter Alternative

* 3 jalapenos diced

* 1-1/2 cups onion diced

* 5 cloves garlic minced

* 20 capers

* 2 cups dandelion greens chopped and packed

* 4 cups kale chopped and packed

* 4 cups collard greens chopped and packed

* 2 cups spinach leaves chopped and packed

* 1/2 cup cilantro chopped and packed

* 1 tablespoon fresh lime juice

* 1/4 cup green food feast powder

* 2 large avocados

* 3 teaspoons Wildly Organic Himalayan Salt or to taste

* 1 teaspoon Wildly Organic Black Pepper

* Wildly Organic Buter Alternative or Wildly Organic Centrifuge-Extracted Coconut Oil add extra as needed

Instructions

1. In a large stock pot, warm the broth to a simmer, then remove from heat.

2. In a separate large skillet or pan, melt the Popcorn Oil.

3. Sauté the jalapenos, onion, garlic, and capers until tender.

4. Next, add the prepared greens (dandelion, kale, collards, and spinach) and seasonings to the pot of warmed broth.

5. Also add the sautéed jalapenos, onion, garlic, and capers.

6. Blend in the pot with an immersion blender or transfer to a stand blender and process in batches. Blend until smooth.

7. Add the avocados and blend again.

8. Add extra Popcorn Oil or Coconut Oil to each bowl before serving, if desired.

Healthy Low Oxalate Bread

Ingredients
* 1 cup water warm
* 2 tablespoons sugar
* 1 packet active dry yeast
* 1 1/2 cup whole wheat flour
* 1/2 teaspoon salt
* 2 tablespoons vegetable oil
* 1 1/2 cup white flour
* 2 tablespoons oatmeal
* 2 tablespoons sunflower seeds

Instructions
* In a large bowl, combine water, sugar, yeast and 1 cup whole wheat flour. Let rest for a few minutes, until bubbles start to form. Add remaining 1/2 cup whole wheat flour, salt and oil.

* Add 1 cup white flour. Mix with a spatula. Pour dough onto floured surface and sprinkle remaining 1/2 cup white flour, oatmeal and sunflower seeds over dough. Knead for 5 minutes, until all the flour, oatmeal & seeds are incorporated and the dough is elastic.

* Rinse large bowl and spray with cooking spray. Place dough in the bowl and cover with a damp towel or plastic wrap. Set bowl in a warm place and let dough rise until doubled in size, about 1 1/2 hours.

* Spray a loaf pan with cooking spray. Punch dough to deflate and shape into a 8-9" log. and place dough into pan. Cover with damp towel or plastic wrap and let rise another 30 minutes. Meanwhile, preheat oven to 375'F.

* Uncover the bread and bake about 30 minutes, until golden brown. To make sure bread is cooked, remove from loaf pan, and gently tap on bottom – the loaf should sound hollow.

* Slice and enjoy

Low Oxalate Ginger Chicken Stirfry

Ingredients

Stirfry Mix

* 1 lb. cooked chicken, dark meat or light meat I like using cooked chicken. It can just be added into the dish and heated through.

* 4 cups purple cabbage, sliced

* 4 cups cremini mushrooms, sliced

* 2 cups peeled carrots

* 3 cups cauliflower florets

* 1/2 cup slant cut green onions

* 1 handful enoki mushrooms

* 2 tbsp vegetable oil

* 1 package rice noodles

Stirfry Sauce

* 4 cloves minced garlic

* 1/4 tsp grated ginger

* 1/4 cup honey

* 1/4 cup rice wine vinegar

* 1 cup chicken stock

* 1 tsp favorite hot sauce (optional)

* 1 tbsp vegetable oil

Instructions

Stirfry Sauce

1. Heat up the oil in a small pot with the garlic. Make sure the garlic is cooked on low to medium heat. You want to make brown sticky garlic, not black.

2. Once the garlic is browned, add in the honey and let bubble for a moment. Then add in the vinegar and cover with a lid to make sure you don't get burned by the bubbling.

3. Add in the chicken stock and reduce by half. Season with salt and pepper and add your favorite hot sauce.

Stirfry Mix

1. Cook the noodles according to the directions on the bag. Drain, cool, and set aside.

2. Heat up the oil in a large wok. Cook the vegetables according to the degree of hardness (cauliflower, mushrooms, cabbage, carrots) and add in the chicken last. The key is to stirfry so make sure not to fill the pan too full. It may be helpful to do the vegetables in batches depending on how big your wok is.

3. Once the vegetables are well caramelized, add in the chicken and noodles and heat through. Add in the stirfry

sauce and mix well. Don't reduce the sauce anymore as it may become too salty. Garnish with green onions and serve

Low Oxalate Smoothie

Ingredients
* 1/2 banana
* 1/2 cup frozen cherries (or other low oxalate fruit)
* 1 tablespoon flaxseed
* 1/2 cup 2% milk (or plain kefir)
* 1/4 cup lowfat plain yogurt

Instructions
* Combine all ingredients in a blender.
* Blend until smooth.
* Enjoy

Delicious Low Oxalate Cabbage Beef Wraps, and the Kidney Stone Diet

Ingredients

Stirfry Sauce

* 2 cups of chopped Shiikate mushrooms

* 1/2 cup of the white part of green onions

* 1 tsp of grated ginger

* 1 tsp of chopped garlic

* 1/2 piece of bacon sliced

* 3 drops of sesame oil

* 1 Tbsp of ketchup

* 1/4 cup of rice wine vinegar

* 1/2 cup of water

* 1 Tbsp butter

* 1 Tbsp of vegetable oil

* Sriracha to spice

Wraps/Rolls

* 1 head of cabbage quartered with stems removed

* 1/2 head of cauliflower grated

* 12 cups of sliced cremini mushrooms

* 1/2 cup of sliced yellow peppers

* 1/4 cup of sliced green onions

* 1/2 tsp of grated ginger

* 1/2 tsp of chopped garlic

* 2 Tbsp of vegetable oil

* Salt and pepper to taste

* 1 lb. of stirfry beef

Instructions

Stirfry Sauce

1. Add the mushrooms, onions, ginger, garlic, and bacon into a pan with the butter and oil and cook on medium heat. You will want to cook these slow so as to develop the most flavor without burning anything. After about 10 minutes, add in the vinegar and reduce by half. Put ingredients into a blender and add the water, ketchup, sesame oil, and salt and pepper to season. Blend until smooth, add in sriracha or any other hot sauce you like to spice things up

Wraps/Rolls

1. Toss the cabbage in vegetable oil, salt and pepper and lay out flat on a baking sheet. Cook for 10 minutes at 350 degrees, or until the edges of the cabbage start to get a bit crispy.

2. Heat up a large pan or wok with the vegetable oil in it. Once the oil starts to smoke a bit add in the beef, vegetables, ginger and garlic and saute until well caramelized. IT would be best to to this in smaller batches to make sure you don't crowd the pan and steam the ingredients instead of stir-fry them.

3. Add in as much sauce as you like. Serve in the cabbage cups and top with extra sauce and chopped green onions. Enjoy.

Low Oxalate Tropical Trail Mix

Ingredients
* 1/2 cup pistachios unsalted, shelled
* 1/2 cup dried cranberries unsweetened
* 1/2 cup banana chips
* 1/2 cup dried mango cut into 1/4 inch pieces
* 1/4 cup coconut shredded or flaked, unsweetened
* 1/4 cup white chocolate chips

Instructions
* Combine all ingredients. Enjoy

Low Oxalate Protein Balls with Cherries and Bananas

Ingredients

* 4 each bananas, peels and cut in half lengthwise

* 4 tbsp butter, room temperature, cut into small cubes

* 1 cup banana chips

* 4 each rice cakes, white or whole wheat

* 1/2 cup raisins, sultana

* 3/4 cup canned cherries, chopped

* 1/2 tsp real vanilla extract

* 1/4 tsp ground cinnamon

* 1/4 tsp cayenne pepper

* 1 each egg white

* 1 scoop vegan protein powder (optional)

Instructions

1. Heat up your oven to the broil setting. Sprinkle the cinnamon and cayenne on the banana halves and put on a baking tray. Broil for 5-7 minutes or until the bananas are well caramelized. Set aside to cool

2. Set the oven to 350 degrees. Blend the bananas with 2 tbsp. of the cubed butter in a food processor until smooth. Set aside.

3. Blend the banana chips in the blender until the desired consistency has been achieved. Add in the rice cakes and pulse until chunky, and not too smooth. Put on a baking tray and bake in the oven until crispy, about 10 minutes.

4. Mix together the banana mixture, and the rice cake mixture with the rest of the ingredients. Mix well to incorporate all ingredients.

5. Make 1-2 oz balls and bake in the oven for 10 minutes until the protein balls have set. Let cool and enjoy

Low-Oxalate, High-Calcium, KETO-Friendly, Grilled Cheese

INGREDIENTS

* 2 ounces of shredded Swiss and Gruyere cheese

* One 16 ounce bag of riced cauliflower

* 1/2 Teaspoon Italian seasoning

* 1/2 Teaspoon of garlic powder

* oil of your choice for pan

* 1 teaspoon of fresh or dried rosemary

* 1/4 cup shredded parmesan cheese

* pepper to taste

* 1 egg

INSTRUCTIONS

1. Take riced cauliflower and put in a food processor to grind it smaller so it looks like sand and can be easily formed into patties. You should get about 2 cups from the 16-ounce bag.

2. Toss the cauliflower into a bowl and add lightly beaten egg, parmesan cheese, Italian seasoning, rosemary, garlic powder, and pepper. Form into what is as close to dough as you can get.

3. Heat a large non-stick skillet over medium-low heat and oil it up. I used canola and a bit of butter. You can use what you like but don't be shy. You don't want the cauliflower "bread" to stick to the pan.

4. Form cauliflower dough into a round patty (you should get 4 patties for two sandwiches). Gently squeeze out any extra fluid from each patty.

5. Place both cauliflower patties into a heated pan for about 5 minutes.

6. Take your spatula and gently flatten each patty and go around and shape into squares that resemble bread.

7. After the 5 minutes are up GENTLY take a spatula and turn the patty over. BE CAREFUL. They fall apart easily at this point.

8. Take 1/2 of the cheese and put it on top of one of the "bread" pieces. Flip the other "bread" slice on top of the cheezed one. Set the timer for 3 more minutes and grill up your sandwich. If your "bread" is not browned keep it on the stove a bit longer.

9. When time is up, gently and carefully take the grilled cheese out of the pan and let it cool on a plate. It will continue to firm up as it cools

Low Oxalate Chicken Jambalaya

Ingredients

Chicken

* 1.5 lbs of chicken breasts

* 1 teaspoon of High Quality Garlic Salt

* 1 teaspoon of Chili Powder

* 1 teaspoon of Montreal steak spice

* salt and pepper to taste

* 2 Tablespoons of Olive Oil

Jambalaya

* 2 cups of White or Wild Rice

* 4 cups of chicken stock

* 1 red pepper 1/4" dice

* 1/4 white onion 1/4" dice

* 1/2 cup of green peas

* 1 teaspoon of Chipotle Powder

* 1 teaspoon of dried basil

* 1 teaspoon of chili powder

* 1 cup of Canned Chopped Tomatoes Organic

* 2 cups of Organic Tomato Sauce

* 2 Tablespoons of Olive Oil

* Salt and pepper to taste

Instructions

1. Cook the rice according to the instructions on the box. Use the chicken stock in place of water.

2. Heat up on high heat a large saute pan with the 2 Tablespoons of olive oil.

3. Season the chicken breasts well with the spices and sear in the pan until golden brown.

4. Add in the peppers, onions, and the jambalaya spices to the pan and put into a 375 degree F oven and cook until the chicken is cooked to 165 degrees F.

5. Take the chicken out of the pan and set aside. Keep warm.

6. Make sure the spices are well cooked out and then add in the chopped tomatoes, tomato sauce, and peas and let come to a simmer.

7. Add in cooked rice and mix together well. Serve on plates with slices of chicken on top.

Harvest Bowl

INGREDIENTS

* 2 cup sweet potato

* 12 ounces sliced grilled chicken

* Freshly ground black pepper

* 2 tablespoon olive oil, divided

* 1/2 lb. broccoli

* 1/4 cup Greek yogurt

* 1 red onion, sliced

* 1/4 cup Dijon mustard

* 1/4 cup unsalted sunflower seeds

* 1 teaspoon dried thyme

* 2 tablespoon sugar-free maple syrup

* 1/4 cup goat cheese

* Freshly ground black pepper

* 1/4 cup white wine vinegar

* 2 cup cooked jasmine rice

* 1/4 cup Trader Joes dried cranberries (or any no sugar added version)

INSTRUCTIONS

1. Preheat oven to 425. On a large, parchment-lined baking sheet, mix broccoli, sweet potato, and red onion with 1 tbsp olive oil. Season with pepper and thyme. Bake for 25-30 minutes until vegetables are tender.

2. Meanwhile, make the vinaigrette. In a large bowl, whisk vinegar, olive oil, greek yogurt, dijon mustard, and sugar

free maple syrup until smooth and combined. Season with pepper.

3. Assemble bowls: top 1/2 cup of rice with 1 cup of roasted vegetables, and 1 cup of chicken. Add cranberries and sunflower seeds to each bowl. Top with a drizzle of dressing, a bit of goat cheese, and serve.

Low Oxalate Green Juice

Ingredients

* 3 Pears Barlett or Williams Green Pears

* 1 Celery 1 stick of celery when juiced is medium oxalate

* 1/4 Cucumber Ths is medium oxalate

* 1/2 Lime

* Ginger A thumb size piece

* Mint A sprig/few leaves

Instructions

1. Peel the lime, leaving the pith intact. This helps to make the juice nice and creamy. The pectin in the pith may also help to enhance detoxification.

2. Push all the ingredients through your vegetable juicer. Ideally place the mint and lime in-between two of the pears of the cucumber as this helps to push it through.

Banookies

INGREDIENTS
* 1 egg
* 1/4 cup coconut flour
* 1/4 teaspoon baking soda
* 1 cup oat flour
* 1/8 teaspoon sea salt
* 1 1/4 cup very ripe banana
* 1/2 teaspoon cinnamon
* 1 tablespoon zero calorie maple syrup

INSTRUCTIONS
1. Heat oven to 350.
2. Add dry ingredients together and mix well.
3. Mash bananas with a fork (it will take about 3 of them) and mix with egg and add to the dry ingredient bowl.
4. Add maple syrup.

5. Mix it all up evenly.

6. Scoop out about 1.5 tablespoons of batter onto a baking sheet (made 8 cookies for me).

7. Bake between 25-30 minutes.

8. Let cool for 10 minutes on wire rack.

9. After totally cool, eat.You can store in the fridge for about 5 days.

Squash Pancakes

INGREDIENTS

* 1 cup Pureed squash acorn or butternut if on a low oxalate diet
* 4 Eggs
* 1 tbsp Coconut oil

INSTRUCTIONS

* Heat pan over medium-low heat. Add oil to melt and coat the pan.
* While waiting for the pan to heat, mix pureed squash and eggs in a food processor or stand mixer (or by hand, in a large bowl, beating with a whisk).

* Pour dollar-pancake sized dollops of the batter into the heated and oiled pan.

* With a flipper, flip the pancakes then the edges begin to crisp. Be sure to cook the pancakes until they are golden on both sides and are fully cooked all the way through.

* Enjoy topped with fruit, nut or seed butter, a drizzle or maple syrup, or your pancake topping of choice

Low Oxalate Green Vegetable Powder

Ingredients

* 6 cups fresh green vegetables choose blend from list above

Instructions

1. Chop the vegetables coarsely.

2. Blanch on the stovetop in boiling water for 3 minutes.

3. Drain/discard the cooking water and immediately rinse the blanched greens in cool filtered water to prevent overcooking.

4. Drain the water again and pat dry gently with a clean, cotton dishtowel.

5. Thoroughly dry the greens in a dehydrator set to 95-105 °F / 35 – 40 °C (preferred method). If you don't have a dehydrator, you can use an oven set to "warm" that goes no higher than 150 °F/ 65 °C (check veggies every hour to avoid over drying).

6. Pulse dried greens in a food processor until desired powder consistency.

7. Refrigerate fresh green vegetable powder in a glass jar with tight lid.

8. Add a teaspoon to each serving of potatoes, eggs, smoothies and soups.

9. Use up within 2 weeks.

Low Oxalate Coleslaw

Ingredients

Salad Mix

* 1/2 head of green cabbage thinly sliced or shredded

* 8-10 radishes thinly sliced

* 1/2 cup of sliced green onions

* 1/2 cup of thinly sliced red onions optional

Dressing

74

* 1/2 cup of high quality mayonnaise

* 2 Tablespoons of grainy dijon mustard

* 2 teaspoons of honey

* 2 Tablespoons of white wine vinegar

* Salt and pepper to taste

Instructions

1. Whisk together the ingredients for the dressing and toss with the salad mix.

2. Mix together well and season with salt and pepper.

Butternut Squash Mac and Cheese (Vegan)

INGREDIENTS

* 400 g cubed frozen butternut squash (roughly 2.5 cups)

* 2 tbsp garlic infused olive oil

* 1 cup oat milk (or other dairy free milk of choice)

* 4 tbsp nutritional yeast

* 1/2 tsp salt

* 150 g gluten-free macaroni (roughly 1.5 cups)

INSTRUCTIONS

* Heat your pan to medium heat and add 2 tablespoons of garlic infused olive oil.

* Add frozen butternut squash cubes.

* Cook until butternut squash is fully thawed and cooked through, stirring often.

* While your butternut squash is cooking, bring a large pot of water to a boil. Salt the water generously and add your gluten-free pasta, stirring often until cooked through. Follow the instructions on the packaging and be careful not to overcook.

* Add oat milk, nutritional yeast and ½ teaspoon salt to your butternut squash.

* Continue cooking until all the flavours have started combining, around five minutes. Stir often. Turn the heat off and let the butternut squash mixture cool down a bit.

* At this point your pasta will likely be done. Strain your pasta and set aside.

* Once your butternut squash mixture has cooled a bit, transfer it into a food processor or blender and blend until smooth.

* Add your sauce to your cooked pasta and stir everything together.
* Serve immediately.

Low Sodium Sloppy Joes

Ingredients
* 1.25 pound ground sirloin
* 2 tbsp low sodium tomato paste
* 1/2 large onion diced
* 1/2 large green bell pepper diced
* 3 cloves garlic minced
* 2 tbsp chili powder
* 2 tsp brown sugar
* 1 1/2 tsp ground mustard
* 1/8 tsp crushed red pepper flakes
* 2 tbsp apple cider vinegar
* 5 tbsp ketchup
* 1/3 cup water

Instructions

* In a large saute pan, brown the ground sirloin. If you don't use lean ground sirloin, drain the excess fat after browning.

* Add tomato paste and cook 1-2 minutes until tomato paste has deep red color. Add onion, green pepper and garlic. Continue to cook 3-5 minutes until vegetables are slightly softened.

* Add remaining ingredients. Mix well. Cover and cook 10-15 minutes.

Low Carb Cauliflower Pizza

INGREDIENTS

* 1 large head cauliflower, grated (about 3 cups), squeezed dry of excess liquid

* 2 1/2 c. shredded mozzarella, divided

* 2 large eggs

* 1 Teaspoon garlic powder

* Freshly ground black pepper

* 3/4 Tomato

* 1 Tablespoon Italian seasoning

* Fresh basil, for garnish

INSTRUCTIONS

1. STEP 1 Preheat oven to 425° and grease a cast-iron skillet with cooking spray. In a large bowl, combine cauliflower, 1 cup mozzarella, eggs, and garlic powder and season pepper.

2. STEP 2 Press mixture into skillet, making sure to get up the sides and bake until deeply golden and dry, 25 minutes.

3. STEP 3 Slice up the fresh tomato and put on top of the crust and sprinkle with the remaining mozzarella.

4. STEP 4 Sprinkle with basil, slice, and serve.

Flax Cracker Crisps- Keto Kidney

Ingredients
* 1/2 cup raw pumpkin seeds
* 1 cup whole flax seeds ground
* 1/3 cup raw sunflower seeds
* 2 teaspoons chia seeds
* 1/2 teaspoon sea salt
* 1 1/4 cups water

Instructions

* Preheat oven to 200°F.

* Cut out parchment paper to line two 11 x 17 inch baking sheets, set aside.

* Add the pumpkin seeds to a food processor and pulse several times, or until the consistency resembles coarse sand.

* Add all the ingredients to a large bowl and stir to combine.

* Place half of the mixture on each baking sheet covered with parchment paper. Lay another piece of parchment paper on top and roll the mixture out evenly. The top parchment paper is key so that the rolling pin doesn't stick.

* Roll the dough thin (about 5 mm) so that the crackers crisp up nicely. Place the parchment paper with the cracker mix onto the baking sheets. Peel off each top piece of paper and discard.

* Cook for 1.5 hours then rotate the pans. If you want to precut the crackers so that they are an even size now is the time. Run a knife or pizza cutter over the dough to outline the crackers. Don't cut all the way through, rather score the dough so that you can break it along the line later.

* Cook for an additional hour. When done the edges will be slightly crispy. Cook an additional 15-30 minutes if needed. Watch closely at the end, the crackers are thin and can burn easily.

* Allow the crackers to cool completely, then break apart.

* Store crackers for up to two weeks in a sealed container.

Roasted Garlicky Brussels Sprouts

Ingredients

* 8 oz (about 25 sprouts) Brussels sprouts trimmed & halved

* 2 Tbs white vinegar

* 2 tsp honey

* 2 tsp Dijon mustard

* 1/8 tsp black pepper

* 1 dash salt

* 1 clove garlic minced

* 2 Tbs olive oil

Instructions

* Place Brussels Sprouts on baking sheet. Recommended: Crowd sprouts ontoone side of sheet to prevent drying out.

* Roast sprouts at 400°F for 20-25 minutes or until fork-tender.

* Meanwhile, combine remaining ingredients.

* When sprouts are done, combine with dressing.

SCD Blueberry Pancakes | SCD, GAPS, Low FODMAP, Low Oxalate

INGREDIENTS

* 3 eggs

* 1 tbsp coconut flour

* ⅛ tsp baking soda

* ¼ cup fresh blueberries

* 1½ tbsp sunflower seed butter May substitute other nut butters if not on low oxalate diet

* 1 tbsp olive oil

* 1 tbsp honey Substitute maple syrup for Low FODMAP

* ¼ cup pineapple juice May substitute with water

INSTRUCTIONS

* Heat a skillet over medium-low heat. Once the skillet is fully pre-heated coat it with a thin layer of cooking oil (non-virgin olive oil works, if that's what you like to use)
* In a blender or food processor, add all the ingredient together and blend until smooth
* Pour a ladle-full of the batter in an even circle in the center of the pan
* Cook for 4 minutes per side

Panzanella Toscana

Ingredients
* 3 tablespoons olive oil
* 4 cups sourdough bread 1" cubes
* 2 large tomatoes 1" chunks
* 1 cucumber 1" chunks
* 1 red bell pepper 1" chunks
* 1 yellow bell pepper 1" chunks
* 1/2 red onion 1" chunks
* 20 fresh basil leaves roughly chopped
* 3 tablespoons capers
* 2 cloves garlic minced

* 1 teaspoon Dijon mustard

* 3 tablespoons white or red wine vinegar

* 1/2 cup olive oil

* 1/2 teaspoon black pepper

Instructions

* Preheat oven to 375'F. Drizzle 3 tablespoons olive oil over bread cubes and place on baking sheet. Bake about 10 minutes, until bread is toasty and slightly browned. Set bread cubes aside.

* Place tomatoes, cucumber, bell peppers, red onion, basil and capers in a large salad bowl.

* Whisk garlic, mustard, vinegar, olive oil and black pepper together.

* Add bread and dressing to salad bowl. Toss to combine. Let sit at least 10 minutes to allow the bread to soak up some of the dressing.

How To Make Healthy Green Smoothies With Superfoods

Ingredients

* 1/4 to 1/3 apple use a green apple for less sugar

* 2" to 3" piece cucumber

* 1 stalk celery

* 1 small to medium carrot

* 1/2 cup fresh parsley chopped

* 1 "puck" pre-steamed then frozen greens or 1 teaspoon fermented kale powder or low-oxalate greens powder

* 1/3 cup berries frozen

* 1/4 to 1/3 cup lemon juice

* 1/4 to 1/3 cup beet juice or 1/2 teaspoon beet powder with 1/3 cup water

* 1 tablespoon raw apple cider vinegar

* 2 tablespoons MCT oil or cream from homemade yogurt, or a combination

* 1 scoop sustainably sourced collagen (certified glyphosate free) save 10% with coupon TCS10

* 1 teaspoon ground turmeric

* 1 teaspoon maca powder red or black

* 1 tablespoon psyllium seed husk

* 1 tablespoon chia seeds

* 1 to 1-1/2 cups yogurt or 1 scoop Vital Whey non-denatured protein powder

* 3 to 4 dropperfuls liquid stevia extract

* additional pure water or homemade cashew milk for consistency

Instructions

1. Load up the Vitamix with ingredients in the order listed, except for the yogurt. It's important to have the soft fruits/veggies at the bottom along with liquids for easy blending. The order of the rest of the ingredients doesn't matter.

2. Blend, starting on low and increasing variable speed until the Vitamix is circulating the foods well.

3. Then flip to high and let fully blend.

4. Now add the yogurt and instead of blending on high, just churn on variable speed 4 to 5 until mixed in. (This prevents your smoothie from getting frothy.)

5. It's best to consume within 20 minutes of making this, so the veggies are at their most potent nutrition.

Warming Low Histamine Chicken Ginger Soup (Low FODMAP, Low Oxalate, Low Lectin)

INGREDIENTS

* 2 Tablespoons Coconut Oil

* 1 Tablespoon Garlic Infused Olive Oil (optional)

* 1 Medium Stalk Celery diced

* 1 Bunch Green Onions, Dark Green Tops Only chopped

* 4 cups Cooked Chicken shredded (about 4 breasts)

* 2 Tablespoons Fresh Ginger finely grated

* 6 quarts Filtered Water

* 4 ounces Baby Arugula

* 6 Medium Carrots chopped into ¼ inch

* 1-2 Rutabagas

* ⅛ teaspoon Redmond Real Salt

* ¼ teaspoon Black Pepper if tolerated

* 2 Tablespoons Cilantro chopped (optional)

* 1 pound Homemade Pork Belly (optional)

INSTRUCTIONS

* If using Pork Belly, follow recipe here and place Pork Belly in oven.

* If you are cooking your chicken at the time you are preparing the soup, start the chicken.

* Cut up the green onions and celery. Grate the ginger.

* On the stovetop, sauté ½ the green onion tops and celery in ghee or coconut oil in an 8 Quart or larger stock or soup pot. About 3 minutes. Add garlic or garlic infused olive oil here, too, if using.

* Add shredded chicken, ginger, sea salt, freshly cracked black pepper, and water to pot. Simmer for 20-30 minutes.

* Meanwhile, peel and cut the carrots.

* Either cube the rutabagas into ½ inch cubes or use a Brieftons Spiralizer to make the rutabagas into noodles.

* Add carrots and rutabaga to pot and continue to simmer on medium heat until tender. About 15-20 minutes.

* Add baby arugula to pot to wilt and turn off stove. Let sit for 5 minutes.

* While arugula is wilting, chop pork belly into bite size pieces (optional). And chop cilantro if using.

* Dish soup into bowls and garnish with green onion tops, cilantro, and pork belly. You could also use fresh parsley if you have it. Then serve and enjoy.

* Freeze the leftovers in Souper Cubes. Freezing leftovers helps to keep histamine levels low.

Baked Honey Garlic Kale Chips (Low Histamine)

Ingredients
* 1 bunch of kale
* 2 teaspoons coconut oil
* 1 Tablespoon honey
* 3 cloves garlic, minced
* Dash of salt

Instructions
1. Preheat the oven to 300°F (150°C). Wash your kale and remove the bulky spines, as they won't cook up nearly as well, and then stack the leaf-halves up and— keeping them stacked together— and fold them in half, crumbling them until they're flexible. Then cut the stack of softened leaves apart; each leaf should end up cut about 10 times (fewer cuts will mean larger chips, and vice versa).

2. Carefully dry your kale and then arrange it in a single layer on one or two baking sheets, drizzle on the coconut oil, and bake for 5 minutes.

3. Meanwhile, measure out the honey and mince the garlic (you can use 1/2 teaspoon garlic powder instead, if tolerated), and then stir the honey, minced garlic, and salt into a chunky paste.

4. Take out your wilted kale and carefully brush on the honey mixture, then bake for 15-17 minutes more still in a single layer. Your chips are done when crispy and just starting to brown.

Stoner Mashed Potatoes

INGREDIENTS

* 2 Tablespoon chives
* 1/4 Cup of skim milk
* 1 head cauliflower
* 1/2 Cup of swiss cheese
* 2 pats of unsalted butter

INSTRUCTIONS

1. Preheat oven to 350 degrees

2. Fill soup pot halfway with water and bring to boil

3. Break up cauliflower into smaller bits and put in pot when water is boiling

4. When cauliflower is soft it is done

5. You can now transfer cauliflower into a food processor or blender. Add the milk (or non dairy milk of your choice), and the butter.

6. When the mixture is creamy transfer cauliflower into a baking dish. Top with swiss cheese and chives. And cover with aluminum foil. Cook for about 10 minutes or until cheese melts.

LOW OXALATE | WHITE CHOCOLATE CHIP COOKIES

Ingredients
* 2 1/2 Cups Oat Flour
* 1 Cup White Rice Flower
* 1 Cup Butter Flavored Crisco
* 3/4 Cup White Granulated Sugar
* 3/4 Cup Brown Sugar

* 2 Egg

* 1 Teaspoon Vanilla

* 1 Teaspoon Baking Soda

* 1 Teaspoon Salt

* 2 Cups White Chocolate Chips

Instructions

1. Pre-Heat Oven to 375 Degrees Mix White Sugar, Brown Sugar, Crisco, and Vanilla until smooth.

2. Add Eggs and mix. In separate bowl stir White Rice Flour, Oat Flour, Baking Soda, and Salt.

3. Gradually add dry ingredients to the wet ingredients.

4. Mix until combined.

5. Mix in White Chocolate Chips until just combined.

6. Scoop dough into 4 ounce balls. Place on cookie sheet.

7. 12 cookies for a standard sized cookie sheet.

8. Bake about 9 Minutes 30 Seconds to 10 Minutes depending on how dark your pan is or how dark you like your cookies.

Low Oxalate Smoothie Recipes

Berry Blast Smoothie

Ingredients:

1. 1 cup mixed berries (strawberries, blueberries, raspberries)

2. 1/2 cup plain Greek yogurt

3. 1/2 cup almond milk

4. 1 tablespoon chia seeds

5. Ice cubes (optional)

Instructions:

1. Blend berries, Greek yogurt, almond milk, and chia seeds until smooth.

2. Add ice cubes if desired and blend again until well combined.

3. Pour into a glass and enjoy immediately.

Green Goddess Smoothie

Ingredients:

93

1. 1 cup spinach

2. 1/2 avocado

3. 1/2 cucumber, peeled and chopped

4. 1 tablespoon fresh mint leaves

5. 1 tablespoon honey (optional)

6. Juice of 1/2 lime1 cup coconut water

Instructions:

1. Blend spinach, avocado, cucumber, mint leaves, honey (if using), lime juice, and coconut water until smooth.

2. Pour into a glass and garnish with a mint sprig if desired.

Tropical Delight Smoothie

Ingredients:

1. 1/2 cup pineapple chunks

2. 1/2 cup mango chunks

3. 1 banana

4. 1/2 cup coconut milk

5. 1 tablespoon flaxseed meal

Instructions:

1. Blend pineapple, mango, banana, coconut milk, and flaxseed meal until smooth.

2. Serve in a chilled glass and enjoy the tropical flavors.

Creamy Almond Butter Smoothie

Ingredients:

1. 1 tablespoon almond butter
2. 1/2 cup unsweetened almond milk
3. 1/2 cup frozen strawberries
4. 1/2 banana
5. 1 tablespoon hemp seeds

Instructions:

1. Blend almond butter, almond milk, frozen strawberries, banana, and hemp seeds until creamy.

2. Pour into a glass and sprinkle with additional hemp seeds if desired.

Citrus Zing Smoothie

Ingredients:

1. 1 orange, peeled and segmented

2. 1/2 cup plain Greek yogurt

3. Juice of 1/2 lemon

4. 1 tablespoon honey (optional)

5. Ice cubes (optional)

Instructions:

1. Blend orange segments, Greek yogurt, lemon juice, and honey (if using) until smooth.

2. Add ice cubes if desired and blend again until well combined.

3. Pour into a glass and enjoy the refreshing citrus flavors.

Blueberry Kale Smoothie

Ingredients:

1. 1 cup fresh kale leaves, stems removed

2. 1/2 cup frozen blueberries

3. 1/2 cup plain Greek yogurt

4. 1 tablespoon almond butter

5. 1 tablespoon ground flaxseed

6. 1 cup unsweetened almond milk

Instructions:

1. Blend kale leaves, blueberries, Greek yogurt, almond butter, flaxseed, and almond milk until smooth.

2. Serve immediately for a nutritious boost.

Vanilla Spinach Smoothie

Ingredients:

1. 1 cup fresh spinach

2. 1/2 cup unsweetened almond milk

3. 1/2 teaspoon vanilla extract

4. 1/2 banana

5. 1 tablespoon sunflower seed butter

Instructions:

1. Blend spinach, almond milk, vanilla extract, banana, and sunflower seed butter until creamy.

2. Pour into a glass and enjoy the subtle sweetness of vanilla.

Mango Coconut Smoothie

Ingredients:

1. 1 cup fresh mango chunks

2. 1/2 cup coconut milk

3. Juice of 1/2 lime

4. 1 tablespoon shredded coconut (unsweetened)

5. Ice cubes (optional)

Instructions:

1. Blend mango chunks, coconut milk, lime juice, and shredded coconut until smooth.

2. Add ice cubes if desired and blend again until well combined.

3. Serve in a chilled glass and garnish with additional shredded coconut if desired.

Raspberry Avocado Smoothie

Ingredients:

1. 1/2 avocado

2. 1 cup fresh raspberries

3. 1/2 cup plain Greek yogurt

4. 1 tablespoon honey (optional)

5. 1 cup almond milk

Instructions:

1. Blend avocado, raspberries, Greek yogurt, honey (if using), and almond milk until creamy.

2. Pour into a glass and enjoy the smooth texture with a hint of sweetness.

Pineapple Mint Smoothie

Ingredients:

1. 1 cup fresh pineapple chunks

2. 1/2 cup fresh mint leaves

3. 1/2 cup plain Greek yogurt

4. Juice of 1/2 lime

5. 1 tablespoon honey (optional)

6. Ice cubes (optional)

Instructions:

1. Blend pineapple chunks, mint leaves, Greek yogurt, lime juice, and honey (if using) until smooth.

2. Add ice cubes if desired and blend again until well combined.

3. Serve in a chilled glass and garnish with a sprig of mint.

Almond Cherry Smoothie

Ingredients:

1. 1/2 cup frozen cherries

2. 1/2 cup spinach

3. 1 tablespoon almond butter

4. 1 tablespoon chia seeds

5. 1 cup almond milk

Instructions:

1. Blend frozen cherries, spinach, almond butter, chia seeds, and almond milk until smooth.

2. Pour into a glass and enjoy the nutty sweetness of almond butter with tart cherries.

Peach Ginger Smoothie

Ingredients:

1. 1 cup frozen peaches
2. 1/2 inch fresh ginger, peeled
3. 1/2 cup plain Greek yogurt
4. 1 tablespoon honey (optional)
5. 1 cup coconut water

Instructions:

1. Blend frozen peaches, fresh ginger, Greek yogurt, honey (if using), and coconut water until smooth.
2. Serve in a chilled glass and enjoy the refreshing flavor with a hint of spice from ginger.

Apple Cinnamon Smoothie

Ingredients:

1. 1 apple, cored and chopped
2. 1/2 teaspoon ground cinnamon
3. 1/2 cup plain Greek yogurt
4. 1 tablespoon almond butter

5. 1 tablespoon flaxseed meal

6. 1 cup almond milk

Instructions:

1. Blend apple chunks, cinnamon, Greek yogurt, almond butter, flaxseed meal, and almond milk until creamy.

2. Pour into a glass and savor the comforting flavors of apple and cinnamon.

Kiwi Spinach Smoothie

Ingredients:

1. 2 kiwis, peeled and chopped

2. 1 cup fresh spinach

3. 1/2 cup coconut water

4. Juice of 1/2 lime

5. 1 tablespoon honey (optional)

Instructions:

1. Blend kiwis, spinach, coconut water, lime juice, and honey (if using) until smooth.

2. Serve immediately for a refreshing and nutrient-packed smoothie.

Carrot Orange Smoothie

Ingredients:
1. 1 large carrot, peeled and chopped
2. 1 orange, peeled and segmented
3. 1/2 inch fresh ginger, peeled
4. 1/2 cup plain Greek yogurt
5. 1 tablespoon honey (optional)
6. Ice cubes (optional)

Instructions:
1. Blend carrot, orange segments, fresh ginger, Greek yogurt, and honey (if using) until smooth.
2. Add ice cubes if desired and blend again until well combined.
3. Pour into a glass and enjoy the vibrant flavors of carrot and orange.

Pomegranate Berry Smoothie

Ingredients:

1. 1/2 cup pomegranate seeds

2. 1/2 cup mixed berries (strawberries, blueberries, raspberries)

3. 1/2 cup plain Greek yogurt

4. 1 tablespoon chia seeds

5. 1 cup almond milk

Instructions:

1. Blend pomegranate seeds, mixed berries, Greek yogurt, chia seeds, and almond milk until smooth.

2. Pour into a glass and indulge in the antioxidant-rich flavors of pomegranate and berries.

Watermelon Mint Smoothie

Ingredients:

1. 2 cups cubed watermelon (seeds removed)

2. 1/4 cup fresh mint leaves

3. Juice of 1/2 lime

4. 1 tablespoon honey (optional)

5. Ice cubes (optional)

Instructions:

1. Blend watermelon cubes, mint leaves, lime juice, and honey (if using) until smooth.

30-Day Nutritional Meal Plan for Low Oxalate Diet

Day 1: Monday

1. Breakfast: Scrambled eggs with spinach and mushrooms.
2. Lunch: Grilled chicken salad with mixed greens, cucumber, and avocado.
3. Dinner: Baked salmon with steamed asparagus and quinoa.

Day 2: Tuesday
1. Breakfast: Greek yogurt topped with fresh berries and a sprinkle of nuts.
2. Lunch: Turkey and vegetable stir-fry with brown rice.
3. Dinner: Beef and vegetable kebabs with a side of roasted sweet potatoes.

Day 3: Wednesday
1. Breakfast: Smoothie with kale, banana, almond milk, and protein powder.

2. Lunch: Quinoa salad with roasted vegetables and feta cheese.

3. Dinner: Grilled shrimp with zucchini noodles and marinara sauce.

Day 4: Thursday

1. Breakfast: Oatmeal with sliced peaches and a drizzle of honey.

2. Lunch: Tuna salad wrap with lettuce and tomato.

3. Dinner: Chicken breast stuffed with spinach and ricotta cheese, served with steamed broccoli.

Day 5: Friday

1. Breakfast: Cottage cheese with sliced pear and sunflower seeds.

2. Lunch: Lentil soup with a side of mixed greens and vinaigrette.

3. Dinner: Baked cod with roasted Brussels sprouts and wild rice.

Day 6: Saturday

1. Breakfast: Whole-grain pancakes with fresh berries and Greek yogurt.

2. Lunch: Spinach and artichoke stuffed chicken breast with quinoa.

3. Dinner: Turkey chili with a side of cornbread.

Day 7: Sunday

1. Breakfast: Smoothie bowl with mango, pineapple, coconut milk, and chia seeds.

2. Lunch: Caprese salad with mozzarella, tomatoes, basil, and balsamic glaze.

3. Dinner: Stir-fried tofu with bell peppers and brown rice.

CONCLUSION

Managing oxalate intake through diet plays a crucial role in promoting kidney health and overall wellness. By adopting a low oxalate diet, individuals can significantly reduce the risk of kidney stone formation, alleviate symptoms of oxalate-related conditions, and maintain a balanced and nutritious diet.

This approach requires thoughtful planning and careful consideration to ensure nutritional adequacy and a varied diet. While there are potential challenges, such as restricted food choices and the need for nutritional vigilance, the benefits of preventing painful and recurrent kidney stones far outweigh these difficulties.

Staying informed about oxalate content in foods, utilizing effective cooking methods, and consulting with healthcare professionals can make managing oxalate intake more manageable. By making health-conscious choices and prioritizing hydration, individuals can support their kidney health and enjoy a higher quality of life.

Made in the USA
Monee, IL
16 November 2024

70309354R00066